Catching the Moon

Catching the Moon

Poems by

Siobhan Farrell

© 2024 Siobhan Farrell. All rights reserved.
This material may not be reproduced in any form, published,
reprinted, recorded, performed, broadcast,
rewritten, or redistributed without
the explicit permission of Siobhan Farrell.
All such actions are strictly prohibited by law.

Cover design by Shay Culligan
Photo by Marty Mascarin

ISBN: 978-1-63980-597-6

Kelsay Books
502 South 1040 East, A-119
American Fork, Utah 84003
Kelsaybooks.com

For Gillian and Corrina

I love you to the moon and beyond . . .

Acknowledgments

Thank you to the following publications, in which versions of these poems previously appeared or are forthcoming:

Coping: "Changing the Script"
Dark Winter: "Freediving"
Dreamers Magazine of Creative Writing: "Dreams Are What We Have Left"
LAIR (Lakehead Arts Integrated Research Gallery): "Coming Home"
NOWW Magazine: "Seeing Orange," "Driving Slow," "Mango Sunrise," "Birds of a Feather," "Beginnings and Endings," "Winter Thoughts," "Driving Home,"
NOWW Magazine (pending publication): "A New Language," "Moving Mountains," "Subway Tokens"
The Prairie Journal of Canadian Literature: "Empty Spaces"
Walleye Magazine: "In Pursuit of Wabi Sabi"

Contents

Rounding the Curve	15
A New Language	16
Awakening	18
Just Run . . .	19
No Endings	20
White Skies	21
Darkness Falling	22
Dream Are What We Have Left	23
Driving Home	25
Farewell Poem	26
Left Behind	27
Distant Footsteps	28
Fence Posts	29
Morning Zazen	31
Seeing Orange	32
Golden	33
Down the Lane	34
Seventy-Four Miles	35
Moving Mountains	36
Walking in Silence	37
Freediving	38
Changing the Script	39
Birds of a Feather	40
Empty Spaces	41
Driving Slow	42
Winter Thoughts	44
Soft Landings	46
Simple Pleasure	47
The Touch of Seasons	48
Time Stood Still	49
Loving Chiang Rai	50
Dancing Shoes	51

Subway Tokens 52
Mango Sunrise 53
Yellow 54
Pursuit of Wabi Sabi 55
Gaia Reclaimed 56
Coming Home 57

Yearning for the Ancient Way

The Way of the Patriarchs coming from the West
I transmit to the East
Yearning for the ancient ways,
Catching the moon, cultivating the clouds
Untouched by worldly dust fluttering about
A thatched hut, snowy evening, deep mountain
　　　—Dogen Zenji, With Hokyoji
(Catching the Moon Mountain, Jewel Mirror Temple)

Rounding the Curve

Heading west chasing clouds
across a cobalt sky, sweat blossoms
against my cheeks.

I'm driving too fast,
jazz spirals up over fields
as I round a long slow curve
into endless space.

No need to straighten my wheel,
just bend into what lies ahead,
everything behind lost in the distance,
the sun hitting me
square in the eyes.

A New Language

I want to soar
swallow-like into the blue,
hold damp petals moist in my palm,
a leaf's crimson veins against my skin,
smooth pebbles to dull
the scratch in my bones.
I want to form new words,
carry them home.

I will live among rocks,
or in fields where bees
turn flowers into honey.
In twilight, the buzz of crickets
will swish grass, an adagio,
each note descending,
fading like breath.

I will read poems
straight from the womb,
translucent tiny stars
among pockets of sand,
pools of water, crimson light
promised a long time ago,
mapped by the moon,
by howls in the night,
lines of people
waving from shore.

It's all a mystery,
these comings and goings,
this worn fabric where
we hold ourselves tight, looking
for something we can call our own.

It could be a dream we once had,
like a shell, a memory
we wear next to our skin, fur
and sinew carved into trees,
twisted roots
that tunnel below us.

So many leaves have fallen on you,
cloaked in yesterday's colours
your eyes like pebbles, like sea glass
under the waves.
I watch you walk out
into deep water.
I will not follow you yet.
I will keep looking for you
elsewhere, perhaps
in our home.

Awakening

It's that time of day
I celebrate most
when silence is held
without judgement
yesterday's worries
are swept out the door
faces are unblemished
by sadness, dreams
swim free
in clear water
and sometimes
that is enough.

Just Run . . .

I don't pretend
that I can make it snow,
change the direction of the wind.

But it's like in grade six
when that red-headed boy chased me home.
I managed to beat him out the door,
knowing I could run faster than all the boys,
faster and faster
till I was safe,
proud and amazed
that I had it in me.

No Endings

Clouds puff up, merge,
grow arms and legs, swirls

of wind blur a vortex
of yellow and red smooth

down onto dappled earth
to land on tunneled roots.

snowflakes
bury berries

once ripened by sunlight
now harvested by the moon

trees freeze white
still rich with life.

White Skies

Snow buntings have returned
to the lake and silent hills,
over fields where frost dusts
tips of grass, sweep upward
between sun and mottled clouds,
into shadowed trees,
alight
on silver branches.

The threat of snow hangs in the air.
I draw up my collar to walk towards
the white blur of home.

Darkness Falling

There is nothing better
than being buried in a field's
ocean of grass in late September,
nowhere to go, nowhere to be
except under the wide sweeping sky,
watching the sun fade into pillowed light,
colours slowly waning, a cow's deep
sweet voice travelling
from a neighbouring field.

I sit doing absolutely nothing,
being nothing but a shadow
as clouds steal across
the land, beauty swept into
rolling tides, pulling
me under as darkness falls
and falls and falls.

Dream Are What We Have Left

Time has mutated
porous
like lichen
on uneven patches of rock,
takes space in cupboards,
with Ritz crackers and old Brie
in the back of the fridge.

Snow windblown whirls
in wanton piles,
crows duel with squirrels
that whiz under trees
around drifts, covering their tracks,
digging to find
underground treasure.

Dusk has turned
moody, spun its own version
of darkness. Days trickle like honey,
unravel with longing for
far-off tomorrows.

Sometime,
late afternoon, I believe
I sip tea with Mum
Dolly Parton, Virginia Woolf
and a team of exhausted
mountain climbers who
somehow made it to the top
no matter what.

Bundled closely,
we inhale the sweet fragrance
of petals, steam rising
from our cups filled
with a perfect blend of jasmine tea.

Driving Home

Your car snowshoed
at least thirty miles under
the speed limit

we were the only people
for miles around

we didn't want
the bends in the road
to straighten

forested hills
to grow into houses

silence
to be filled.

Farewell Poem

When I told you I was leaving
you told me that sometimes
you get lonely,
that you love to watch
hundreds of fireflies
in the fields behind your house.

Then you asked me to write
you a poem about fireflies.

Left Behind

When I wake up
in the half-dawn light
you are dead.

When I eat my lunch,
there you are,
dead again.

When I sip my red wine at dinner
which you liked so much,
you are still dead.

And when I finally crawl
numb and tired into bed,
you are not sleeping,
but dead.

Distant Footsteps

Winter treads soft as a shadow,
snowflakes nudge branches,
clings cold to fingertips.

Silence hangs deep,
sun's breath flows
downward
awakening leaves
shaking them loose.

My footsteps
stamp into remnants of snow,
the moon lingers, falls
into my waiting arms.

New life has entered my bones,
interrupting conversations
I've wanted to have,
now just dreams under my pillow.

Soil gathers
under the soles of my feet
I listen to frogs, crickets
the music of rivers,
the chatter of ducks.

I remember your footsteps
alongside mine,
just not all of the time.

Fence Posts

Fallowed fields tinged with frost,
winter light blurs
into pillowed embers.

In stillness, my eyes are drawn
to what jumps furthest
fastest.

Squirrels don't think
or measure,
they just leap

from drooping birches to fence posts
across space, never once missing
their target.

They scramble up trunks
hiss, threatening me
with their absurd
puffed up tails.

Swallowed by darkness,
I feel small
and vast, winds soften
my face.

Figures shuffle by
dogs, strollers, fluffy jackets
skirting me as I walk past.
It is the skirting that makes me sad,
the young who have made me old.

Tomorrow chattering squirrels,
will likely mock me again.
I wouldn't expect anything else.

Morning Zazen

The bell rings three times
for four am zazen.

Dim light and silence
calm my pounding heart.

Breathe in, breathe out,
clarify the mind.

Tears and snot drench my sleeves,
yet joy inhabits me too.

Seeing Orange

Sometimes I wonder why I drive for twelve hours
into rural Iowa for five days to join
a constellation of tents
in a tick-infested field where each night
I lay my unenlightened mind,
and each morning rise to sit cross-legged
in silence, to stare at white zendo walls,

I accept that after endless days exploring
empty canyons, each restless night
dissolves into a familiar place
where I yearn to lose myself in the arms of the shiny tin man
with the voice like a broken teacup who has broken
my heart for the very last time.

One sun-drenched afternoon, holding a black walnut
in my palm under the shade of a cottonwood tree,
I see and am seen by a bright orange towel
on a clothesline swaying in a long slow dance.
This sunrise of fabric invites me to spread
colour across the sky, under the sun,
then the moon and the stars.

Golden

Buried in a field of barley
under a waterfall of golden light,
reciting promises of a life to be lived,
cherishing the land
and each other, together
for that brief and tender moment.

But she has no memory of it,
it's just a photo she studies, wondering
who was that woman
with arms outstretched,
so sure of herself,
knowing everything except
who was that man
holding the camera.

Down the Lane

The moon hung veiled in cloud,
but my feet know their way
down the lane towards
a silhouette of a house nestled
in the crumbling hill,
layers of rock and earth
sheltered under a birch canopy,
surrounded by blue spruce
we had planted
together.

I imagine you
making dinner,
washing dishes,
our daughters spread on the carpet
watching TV in the room's soft glow,
surrounded by African curios and plants
spilling over leather couches starting to wear
thin after a life within these walls.

Rooted in silence,
all hurt dissolve into a place
where my heart wants to rest,
to join this conversation,
this circle
that was once my family,
that was once my home.

Seventy-Four Miles

I'm trying not to hold too tightly
to these seventy-four miles between
Superior and Bayfield Wisconsin
beside my ninety-two-year-old mother

who stares out her window
between nods of sleep,
listening to Yo Yo Ma
playing bluegrass.

Clouds unfurl, the sun
beats in our eyes.
We ride alongside wildflowers,
the smell of the wind.

Hawks circle and circle,
hay bales like nests,
giant furry animals
doze warm in the fields.

I know that summer will end,
snowbirds will swoop down.
I know this seat beside me
will one day be empty.

I know these seventy-four miles
are a gift,
a journey
we are making together

towards the big lake
stretching out as the sun
sinks in the sky
and finally sleeps.

Moving Mountains

This morning you scaled the Thorong La Pass
in your Doc's slushing through
ice and snow,
winds whipping prayer flags
and strands of your hair.

I walk in meditation deep
in the boreal forest, a cool wind
blowing in from Lake Superior.

I circle the pine knotted floor,
on the path beside you
where I walked thirty years ago.

Walking in Silence

Wildness has entered this
space above granite rock,
the song of the winter wren
fills me, my body weaves
through shifting shadows.

Sunlight pierces dusty windows,
a raven carves itself into a knothole,
prayer flags flutter, diffused by crimson
light that grows into trees,
petals blossom from the floor.

Warmth filters through
branches, countless stars swim
through my veins, ancient fossils
and fine sand rust my bones,
my foot hovers, forever
in this golden moment.

Freediving

It's no use to swim
without water.
Nothing will keep you afloat.
Under you, a murky

bottom, impossible
to rise through
strangling
strands of algae.

It's like pacing back and forth
on a slimy beach scattered
with crayfish, crabs,
waiting for the high tide,
to carry you out to sea.

Just plunge into icy blue
swing your arms wild,
slide jelly-like
through that deep hum of space
shedding layers of skin as you
dive deeper and further
away from shore.

Changing the Script

My life is improvised-
a foul cabal of cells has
destroyed innocent tissue,
my body repossessed,
rivers diverted to flood
vast territories.

But it's not what you think . . .
my body is not a battlefield.
I get that you want to take sides.
but both sides are mine and mine alone.

I reject your litany of prognoses,
prescriptions and pronouncements.
I want to hold the darkness in my hands
and taste the sweetness
of my wild and wondrous life.

Birds of a Feather

I'm crying again. Yellow
leaves spiral down,
cling frozen to my car.
A lone sea gull,
wings stretched wide, splashes
against the darkening sky.

I'm listening to Stacy Earle,
played her at least fifteen times
the last few days, listening
to the same tunes
over and over.
I like that they make me sad.

I'm trying to remember
the sound of my legs
swishing through grass,
tickling my thighs.

Hundreds of geese claim
their space in the sky, carving
the air with their sound.
The universe is open to them,
yet there is only direction,
they know exactly
where they will land.

Empty Spaces

Opening our eyes, tears stream down
faces, pain spilling between gulps
of air from the new arrival
still smelling of booze,
bruised interlaced cuts streaked
across her face and hands,
clenched eyes,
perched on her plastic chair
rocking back and forth.

Her story gets patched into
the collection of tragedies
that bind these repeat visitors of
every program, every cell,
courtroom and dark alley where
poisons are horse traded to numb
the mind, to maim and kill
what remains of their hearts
after blow after savage blow.

Now we simply sit, the rhythm
and wisdom of our bodies and minds
in this act of love, of rebellion,
tearing apart any pretense,
any last piece of bullshit,
a brave circle of women
breathing in breathing out together
in this grey hushed basement room.

Driving Slow

Driving slow bumper to bumper
flat-iron frozen by sombre chill,
Labour day just behind us but
feeling like the dregs of October.

We're back in the game.
The brutal necessity of the hunt
spewing ash over houses, trees,
hunched helmeted cyclists
and troops of windblown children.

Brittle poplar leaves with
hints of red blow madly, half terrified
off branches, early frost blows out
each last flickering flame.

We're trying so hard to be brave,
inching along under clouds
like a Monet painting,
pale, tired and unwashed,
it simply breaks my heart.

I'm wedged behind another fucking
black truck with a silver ram
nailed to its rear end,
tires spinning,
going nowhere.

I'm just waiting
for the light to change,
for life to overflow its banks
instead of counting it
minute by minute
season by season
heading somewhere alone
in my car.

Winter Thoughts

Why did I start thinking about salamanders?
I have no particular interest in amphibians
or reptiles for that matter.

They're a cross between lizards and frogs,
with long tails and four legs
or only two.
They even eat meat,
which is somehow scary.

It's true when I was five
I collected frogs and plopped them
into an old bathtub
crusted with algae.

 I saw a rattler in a dinosaur park,
ran over a white python in South Africa,
reluctantly picked up grass snakes
from time to time.

I have shared rooms with geckos
as they see-sawed up and down
smooth walls catching mosquitoes.
As long as they kept their distance,
I kept mine.

I love the deep voices of bullfrogs
croaking in unison,
telling me everything will be fine.

Salamanders are blissfully yellow
or orange and slimy,
they dart though sweaty leaves
fallen logs, and soft brown earth,

their smooth skin, dark beady eyes
blinking against the sun.

Salamanders couldn't live
this far north,
their skin would crack,
they would soon go hungry,
while snakes and frogs know quite well
when to bury themselves under the snow.

Soft Landings

My feet travel across wide rivers
of ice stretched across a trail
as I try to anchor myself
on twisted roots of spruce and cedar.

Leaping from patches of dirt
side to side
treading ever so slowly,
clumsy, anxious,
breathless
trying not to fall

Until like an animal,
I no longer check
where my feet should land,
they figure it out on their own.

Sometimes you just need to remember
what your body already knows.

Simple Pleasure

After two glasses of red wine
my flannel sheets warm
soft and clingy,

my shiny black cat
jumps up, dumps
his whole fifteen pounds
onto my left foot,
I couldn't be happier.

The Touch of Seasons

In the last days of summer,
clouds are hued with loneliness.
shadows etch stones, bearing witness,
darkness sweeps crimson hills
into the sea, silence spreads
deep beneath stone,
amongst fallen leaves.

Yet decay has its own perfection.
there is no need to mourn
the passing of flowers,
Their scent will linger
into the night.

Time Stood Still

A small boy in love
with swimming
laughs as he paddles by,
a heron whooshes
high above him.

My legs loosen
on the cool hard dirt,
pale legs soft,
ghostly toes spread wide,

I sink into languid heat,
the world loose
upon my shoulders.

Warm air is so blue
it stops time long enough
for me to look away
and turn back

to hear the splash of the boy,
catch the blur of heron dive
into the waves,
for my tears
to become sunlight.

Loving Chiang Rai

Morning heat irons the dusty road,
sweat snakes slow smooth
down my skin like oil.
Sun's glare creeps into houses,
crumbling offices, sluggish gardens
where blooms droop in defeat.

I want to catch up to giggling
children in starched uniforms,
dangling their satchels.
Heads flung high, their loud voices
hoot flash
zig zag
in front of them.

I want to run my fingers
through their jet-black hair,
feel their joy against my skin.

Dancing Shoes

Killing my last few hours in Beijing
under lychee branches
by the Imperial Gardens.

The day is still unblemished.
Smells of rice and dust mingle
with cedar and wild roses.
Morning heat bruises doorways
of dumpling and noodle shops.

Street sweepers clean debris
after last night's rain.
Cars bleat, bikes claim space,
soldiers stand at attention beside
girls giggling in rainbow dresses.

A father buys his daughter
a wand. She twirls it round
and round, her red dress
and pigtails whirl
faster and faster,
pure joy in each spin
of her shiny black pointed shoes.

Subway Tokens

A pharmacist
at four am with a broken debit machine
took my three subway tokens
to pay for drugs.
How can life get any better?

Mango Sunrise

Nothing clears your head
like a July morning jumbled
yawning wedged
on your doorstep
beside your cat washing his paws.

Slices of mango
like blossoms on your Mexican
hand-painted turquoise plate
with the dancing peacock
you fell in love with long ago.

Freshly mown grass curves up trunks
into a sheen of blue and green.

You sip coffee,
slip a piece of mango past your lips,
let its juice trickle down your chin.

Everything in you is warm,
like sunrise.

Yellow

Yellow is the colour of happiness,
daffodils pushing through soil,
sunshine spilling
into rocks and crevices.

Yellow is the colour of hooded raincoats,
rubber boots worn
by young explorers
sloshing through rain puddles

Yellow and black fuse together
in the furred coat
of the honeybee, drawing
sweet nectar onto our tongues.

Yellow is the colour of sadhus
in saffron robes whose
prayers remind us
of what we could be.

Yellow is fun-loving
reckless and adventurous,
yellow is my younger
and braver self.

Yellow is the promise
that life will triumph,
fear and doubt are a dead end,
the golden road is there for the taking.

Pursuit of Wabi Sabi

Forgive yourself,
your lapses of judgement,
binge watch Friends,
leave last night's dishes,
wear week-old PJ's
ignore emails, texts,
advice from afar.

Find beauty in your imperfection,
in your scarred flawed stained
well-used life.
Ignore the wreckage,
the empty beer cans,
make friends with that face
in the mirror,
the unruly mind
that won't be tamed.

Give in to the chaos, regrets
treasure your one life
that strews bliss
and heartache.

Embrace wabi-sabi.
Become broken,
become human.

Gaia Reclaimed

My eyes have grown tired,
lost their focus,
drawn to the slow burn,
tinges of light, earth's rotation
through space.

Closing my eyes,
I rest in silken water,
a sheen of beaded stars
not bound by rules or muffled
by the maelstrom of waves
that roll into shore.

Still, there is the clamour of rain,
crunch of bones, slap of bodies
washing up on the shore,
the weeping
of those who cannot bear to give birth,
of those who have turned away,
that can no longer hope.

Yet consciousness is permeable,
even infinite.
Clouds can be parted,
we can unfurl pebbles
one by one.
feel our broken bodies
ripen, paint a vision
of rapture.

Coming Home

The lilacs are almost spent
but their fragrance catches in my throat
after the last leg of my journey over the Arctic Ocean
into Hudson's Bay and the forest-hewn city
on the edge of the boreal forest,
far from Asiatic winds,
and the lemony scent of frangipanis.
I left my daughters on a small island
where we had explored vast geographies,
climbed hills cloaked in light and shadowed bamboo,
sipped fruity concoctions in beach cafes, wandered
through markets with too many cats, got lost
on untidy streets draped in saffron robes
and Superman T-shirts.
We floated on waves
distant drums, fireflies, lightning
filled the sky.

Frost-tinged green
feels soft against my skin.
I want to let the earth disappear
below my feet,
become the sun filled sky,
cradle the fish and the birds,
and everything else is unimportant.

About the Author

Siobhan Farrell was born in England, grew up in Toronto, and now lives in Thunder Bay, a small city on the north shore of Lake Superior deep in the boreal forest. Her work is influenced by the wondrous power of nature, beauty inherent in many forms of artistic expression, and *Wabi Sabi,* a Japanese term which means finding beauty in imperfection. She lives with her black cat Mizuki and too many plants. This is her first collection of poems.

www.ingramcontent.com/pod-product-compliance
Lightning Source LLC
Chambersburg PA
CBHW030915170426
43193CB00009BA/864